CONTENTS

Introduction

The aim of this handbook is to provide information and practical guidance for those working with people who self-injure. It has been written for the many professionals and voluntary workers who come across people who deliberately hurt themselves in various ways.

Self-injury is far more common than is generally realised. Those working in settings as diverse as hospitals, GP surgeries, community mental health services, schools and colleges, social services, prisons, children's homes, drug and alcohol projects, supported housing and many more are likely to encounter people who harm themselves. Yet most professional training provides little or no preparation for working with self-injury. There is often little guidance or information available for those wishing to help someone who self-injures. And there may be a lack of support for workers dealing with the difficult feelings and issues this work can raise.

This handbook begins by providing some background information about self-injury. It goes on to explore the impact and implications of working with self-injury for professionals and helpers. The rest of the book is concerned with providing a helpful basis for effective working: understanding of self-injury, knowledge about ways of helping, and ideas on providing for the needs of staff and practitioners in this field.

For anyone who'd like to know

*For anyone who'd like to know, these are some of the things I wou...
to hear when I se njure:*

You must be feelin a lot of pain to do this to yourself.

I understand that your injury hurts.

I accept that you need to do it at the moment.

*I would like to listen if you would like to tell me why you needed to do it
this time.*

I am not labelling you or judging you.

I see you as more than just your self-harm.

What, if anything, can I do to help you right now?

I care about you.

I care about your injury but I'm not panicking.

I still respect you.

Your body is your responsibility, I won't try to stop you or take control.

It's okay to tell me what you did.

I can cope with your pain and your injury.

Would you like me to hold your hand?

You deserve to be loved and cared for.

From a SHOUT reader

With thanks to SHOUT magazine and to the anonymous reader who
contributed these words.

Chapter 1
About self-injury

What is it?

Self-injury is any act which involves deliberately inflicting pain and/or injury to one's own body, but without suicidal intent. The most common form of self-injury is cutting, often of the arms and hands, perhaps of the legs, and less commonly of the face, stomach, back, hips and bottom, or genitals. Some people burn or scald themselves, others inflict blows on their bodies, or bang themselves against something. Sometimes people inflict different sorts of injury upon themselves at different times, depending upon their feelings and what is available to them.

Other ways people injure themselves include scratching, picking, biting, scraping, and occasionally inserting sharp objects under the skin or into body orifices. Less common forms of self-injury include pulling out one's hair and eyelashes and scrubbing oneself so hard as to cause abrasion, (sometimes using cleansers such as bleach). Some people swallow sharp objects or harmful substances. Others tie something tightly around a part of their bodies.

Shocking though it can be to hear or read about, it is important to recognise that most self-injury is not severe. Most people who hurt themselves do so quite superficially and carefully, and although scars may often be left, no serious long-term damage is done. A small minority of people, however, do harm themselves more severely and dangerously. Many people deal with their injuries themselves, although some seek treatment from Accident and Emergency departments.

How common is self-injury?

To date no studies of self-injury have been carried out in the general population, so that it is not possible to be sure how many people hurt themselves in this way. Estimates have suggested that at least 1 in 600 people injure themselves sufficiently to need hospital treatment (Tantam & Whittaker, 1992). This excludes those (probably many) who present their injuries as accidental. There is considerable under-reporting, with many people hiding self-injury even from their families, and never coming to the attention of health practitioners. Confidential helplines receive calls from people who have injured themselves for years without telling anyone, due to shame and fear of condemnation. It seems likely, therefore, that self-injury is far more common than is generally realised.

Who self-injures?

Under-reporting makes it difficult to provide accurate information about the sorts of people who injure themselves. Self-injury is commonly reported amongst psychiatric patients and prisoners. It is also well-known amongst people with learning disabilities and other conditions, such as autism.

Self-injury in such populations is far more likely to be detected than that carried out by people living, coping and holding down jobs in the community. Agencies offering confidential support can provide some useful clues. Voluntary support agencies, University counselling services and independent counsellors and therapists all report that they encounter self-injury amongst people who are apparently functioning extremely well, perhaps pursuing professional careers, bringing up children, and so on. It seems likely that many more such people are injuring themselves but are currently failing to come to the attention of any support agencies.

It seems that self-injury is more common amongst women than amongst men. This difference is likely to reflect the different pressures and expectations placed on men and women in our society. (Women often feel conflict about their bodies. They are also more likely to turn feelings such as anger upon themselves.) Where men self-injure it is usually when they have less power than is usual for men (such as in prison).

Self-injury most often begins in adolescence, although for some it starts in earlier childhood. Some people do not start injuring themselves until they are adults.

Often people report that their self-injury began in childhood, with scratches and bumps being disguised as 'accidents'. They progressed to more systematic cutting, burning and so on in adolescence. It is important that professionals working with children and young people are aware of self-injury, so that the problem can be picked up quickly. This is especially important given that self-injury almost always occurs in response to serious problems such as abuse in a young person's life.

Self-injury is often seen as a problem affecting younger adults and it is less often reported amongst people of middle age and later years. However, we know that self-injury sometimes carries on for many years, so that older adults must also be harming themselves. It is not yet clear whether the apparent rarity of self-injury amongst older people is real (perhaps because people stop self-injuring as they mature), or whether the difference is due to underreporting. It may be that the stigma and shame associated with self-injury (and the problems underlying it) affect reporting by older people even more. Again, this may lead to a failure to identify and respond to people's distress.

How often do people self-injure?

People vary in terms of how frequently they hurt themselves. Some people only injure themselves every few months. For others, self-injury is a regular part of their lives, the way they cope from week to week or even day to day.

Most people go through periods of hurting themselves more often when they are under some particular stress. Some people, for example, may normally manage to go for several days or weeks before their feelings build up sufficiently to drive them to self-injure. But at difficult times they may hurt themselves every day. Someone who has not self-injured for some years may find herself using this coping strategy again for a while if something particularly distressing happens in her life. It is useful for workers to be aware of such patterns so that they do not panic when self-injury escalates, but can help a person to identify what has caused this and to have access to appropriate support for a while.

Self-injury and suicide attempts

Understandably, many people assume that when a person injures themselves they are making a suicide attempt, or at least a suicidal gesture. However, self-injury is not the same thing as a suicide attempt, in fact it is usually something very different: a desperate attempt to cope and to stay alive in the face of great emotional pain. (Much more will be said about the reasons people self-injure in Chapter 3).

The difference between self-injury and a suicide attempt may not be apparent to others, since often the same sort of injury (such as cutting of the wrist area) could be interpreted in either way. However most people who self-injure, if asked, are very clear that what they are doing is not a suicide attempt.

They do not wish to die, only to rid themselves of unbearable feelings. Even so, sometimes an individual may feel confused about their own motivation for hurting themselves. They may need to talk through what has happened and what led up to it before they can clarify for themselves that their intention was not to die, but to try to deal with their desperation.

Professionals may fear that a person who self-injures is close to suicide. While self-injury is **not** about suicide, someone who hurts themselves is usually in deep distress. Like anyone else in distress they are more likely than normal to kill themselves. However, it is very important not to panic, and to remember that someone who self-injures is in fact trying to cope and carry on with life. It is quite likely that they have been coping in this way for many years, without seriously endangering their own life.

Self-injury and other self-harm

Inflicting wounds and injuries is of course not the only way in which people may harm themselves. Self-injury can be seen within a much broader context of self-harm, which includes things as diverse as:

abuse of alcohol, drugs, solvents; drug overdoses

smoking

starving, bingeing, vomiting, compulsive eating, over-exercising;

engaging in dangerous or unwanted sex

staying in abusive or unsatisfactory relationships (n.b. there may be little choice about this)

self-isolation

risk-taking, putting oneself in dangerous situations

driving too fast or when drunk

self-neglect

getting into fights; getting into trouble with Police

gambling, habitual over-spending

being 'selfless' - consistently putting one's own needs last

guilt, worry, self-denigration, perfectionism

habitual overwork, over-ambition/under-ambition

It is useful to place self-injury within this wide context of self-harm, in order to help our understanding. Although self-injury has its own very specific meanings for an individual, the problems and motivations beneath self-injury are often similar to those underlying other, more familiar sorts of self-harm. Some of our understanding of these can therefore be applied to self-injury. For example, in the same way that one person may use drugs or drink to escape their feelings, so another may be able to distract herself from her emotional pain by hurting her body.

Seeing self-injury within a much wider context also helps us to recognise that it is not such an alien thing as it may at first seem. In fact most of us sometimes behave in ways which are harmful to ourselves. Often this will involve something socially acceptable, such as smoking, overworking, or always putting others first. Yet these may also be quite harmful to us in the long-term. Our reasons for doing these things can also help to shed light on what may drive someone else to self-injure. For example, smoking may relieve tension, while overworking or over-concern for others may help someone to avoid feelings of unhappiness about their own life. Similar motivations can also be involved in self-injury.

Chapter 2

Issues and challenges for workers

Working with people who self-injure inevitably raises many difficult issues and feelings. In this chapter we identify many of these and go on to consider how they may influence our responses to clients.

Feelings

Self-injury naturally arouses many uncomfortable feelings, however professional we are. We would have to be inhuman not to experience strong reactions, which may include:

Shock, horror and disgust

When a worker first encounters someone who self-injures they often feel deeply shocked and disturbed. It can be horrifying and traumatic to see or even hear about a person's wounds or scars. These natural reactions don't necessarily go away with more familiarity, and feelings of horror and perhaps disgust may arise every time a worker encounters a new incident or form of self-injury.

Incomprehension

Feelings of shock are often closely followed by incomprehension. "How could anyone do that to themselves?" "Why on earth do they do it?" Most people then go on to search for some sort of explanation. They need to find some way of explaining something so unsettling, of making it into something they can understand and cope with more easily.

Fear and anxiety

It is natural for us to react with alarm to seeing or hearing about injury and blood. The wounds themselves may be worrying, and even if these are dealt with safely a worker may be frightened by the knowledge that a person can do such things to themselves. They may also fear what the person may do next. Will they harm themselves more seriously, or even kill themselves?

Distress and sadness

"You try not to show it, but sometimes you just feel so sad, knowing what someone's been through, and then they're hurting themselves on top of it. And the scars will be there forever."

Working with a person who self-injures may be very upsetting. A worker or helper may feel distressed about the injuries and scars on the body of a person they have come to care about. They may also feel sad about the emotional pain behind the self-injury. Self-injury cannot easily be ignored, it shouts to us of someone's distress. It may also remind us uncomfortably of some of our own pain and sadness, the hurts in our own lives.

Anger and frustration

Hard though it may be to admit, it is natural to sometimes react to self-injury with anger and frustration. Anger can be a response to the feelings of shock, fear and upset discussed above. It can help us to feel less powerless.

Workers may feel angry and frustrated with a client who self-injures, particularly if they have put a lot of time and care into working with them. They may also feel anger towards the people in the person's life who have caused the distress underlying the self-injury. Some people also feel frustrated by working within a system which often fails to recognise and respond to the distress of people who self-injure.

Powerlessness and inadequacy

Those working with people who self-injure often report feeling powerless and helpless. They are desperate to help and to 'do something', and yet their efforts may appear to have little effect. This can lead them to lose confidence and to feel therapeutically useless, and perhaps guilty. They come to believe that the person cannot be helped, or that they themselves do not have the skills or knowledge to do so.

These feelings arise very naturally in a context where self-injury is poorly understood, and workers are not adequately trained and supported for this work. Many people also work in settings where the viability and success of their work with clients are measured by observable improvement, which is expected to occur within a relatively short time. This is problematic since self-injury often continues for many years, and can be very difficult to give up. A person may make considerable improvements in her life and yet continue to hurt herself. This means that helpers may be doing very good work with a client, but they or others may not recognise the value of the work, in the face of the continued self-injury. This can be very disheartening.

Issues and dilemmas

Responsibility and accountability

A worker may also feel a frightening degree of responsibility for someone who self-injures. If a person they are working with hurts themselves, they may wonder if it is somehow their fault. Did they miss a problem, or do something to upset them? Will they be held accountable? Workers in some settings, of course, actually have statutory responsibility for the safety of clients, and may be held accountable if someone in their care comes to serious harm. Others without such responsibility may still see it as part of their job to prevent someone from hurting themselves.

Professional dilemmas

Working with someone who self-injures can present the helper with some serious dilemmas. It may be difficult for them to reconcile their concerns about responsibility and accountability with their desire to allow clients privacy and autonomy.

"I know it's a coping strategy, but it's hard to stand back and let someone cut themselves when you're worried about them, and about your boss coming down on you like a ton of bricks."

Some professionals (such as those working in prisons and hospitals) are required to report and take action concerning self-injury or even the risk of it. This can seriously interfere with their efforts to build a trusting alliance with the person in their care.

Further, self-injury often escalates for a while during therapeutic work, when the person is confronting the very experiences and feelings which have caused her to cope in this way. Anxiety about this may lead a worker to shy away from addressing important material with their client.

Expectations

Another pressure which workers may face is the expectation from a client's family and from other professionals that they should be able to stop someone from injuring themselves. It can be hard for people to understand that self-injury will not just go away, if only the professionals involved would do their job properly. Workers in this field need to come to terms with the fact that there is no simple 'cure' for self-injury, and that they themselves may be scapegoated for failing to find one.

Conflicting approaches

The situation of workers grappling with this problem is made worse by the fact that there is little guidance available, let alone consensus on how best to treat someone who self-injures. There may be sharply conflicting views within and between groups of professionals as to what approach should be taken.

"I try to do what feels right to me but I get worried that nobody will back me up if things go wrong, because other staff tend to play safe."

Such conflict can lead to staff feeling criticised, isolated and unsupported. It can make team and co-working difficult.

Effects of self-injury on others

A worker may have to deal with the effects of a person's self-injury on other clients, and/or on their partner, family and friends. Such people are likely to be upset, frightened, resentful and angry about the self-injury.

'Contagion'

"Sometimes it seems like all it takes is for one person to cut themselves and then all hell breaks loose and we're stretched to our limits, trying to cope."

Those working in residential, inpatient, or any other group settings may have to deal with the fact that self-injury seems to sometimes happen in 'rashes'. This can lead to the suspicion that clients are copying or 'catching' self-injury from one another. Workers may feel angry with the person starting off the 'rash', or with clients they perceive as copying, seeking attention, and not really 'needing' to self-injure. The situation can become chaotic, with staff struggling to cope and to deal with what is happening.

Getting it right

There can be a lot of anxiety about how to 'get it right' when working with someone who self-injures. Particular concerns might include uncertainty about how to react to someone hurting herself or disclosing that she does so, and fear that what one says will somehow make the self-injury worse.

Implications for work with people who self-injure

It is natural and understandable for someone working with people who self-injure to struggle with many of the feelings and issues discussed above. What needs to be considered next is how these feelings and issues may impact on our work. Sometimes the stress and difficulties of dealing with self-injury and our own reactions to it can lead us to work in ways which are not very helpful. This is particularly so if we do not have sufficient support and supervision for our work.

Avoidance

One possible response to the difficult feelings and issues which self-injury raises may be to turn away from the person we are working with. We do not want to see their injuries, or what these tell us about the extent of their pain. We may protect ourselves by dismissing or ignoring the person. We call what they are doing 'silly', or 'a phase'.

Linked to not wanting to know is avoidance of working with people who self-injure altogether. We argue that self-injury can only be dealt with by some other 'expert'. When cases come up for allocation we hope fervently that someone else will take them on. So we are robbed of the chance to offer the very real help that we are in fact able to give.

Many residential projects, counsellors, psychologists, groups, etc. exclude people who self-injure. This means that there are few services available, leaving those of us who do work with people who self-injure feeling burdened and isolated.

Bad or mad

One very human response to the distress and uncertainty self-injury causes us can be to condemn the person who hurts herself. "She's only got herself to blame", "he doesn't want to get better", "don't they realise how much it upsets other people?". People who self-injure report being called 'selfish', 'childish', 'disgusting' and many other very hurtful things by staff they encounter in various services. Clearly this is not helpful - such reactions compound the self-hatred and isolation which lead someone to self-injure. And often we ourselves do not really feel comfortable with such responses.

Another way in which we may seek to distance ourselves from someone who self-injures (and thus from the difficult feelings we experience) is by deciding that they are ill or disturbed. Unfortunately, once someone is seen as 'disturbed', workers may believe they cannot understand them, and tend not to take what they say seriously. Meanwhile the person who has been labelled may react with fear and anger, or by giving up her own sense of power and responsibility for her own life. Our ability to work effectively together is seriously undermined.

Simplistic explanations

The discomfort and incomprehension which self-injury causes in helpers can lead us to seek hasty and over-simple explanations. It is understandable that we feel the need to grasp at some way of comprehending what shocks and disturbs us, yet in doing so we can miss out on the deeper and more satisfactory understanding that time and reflection could provide. This problem is compounded by the fact that there is little training or literature available about self-injury, and little enlightened discussion of the issue. In this vacuum, myths and assumptions about what leads someone to self-injure can have great power.

The most commonly held motivations attributed to people who self-injure are probably 'attention-seeking' and 'manipulation', both of which usually imply disapproval. As will be seen in Chapter 3, the motivations for self-injury may be extremely complex and subtle, and can vary considerably from person to person, or from time to time in the same person's life. It is much harder for us to live with the uncertainty and complexity which this knowledge can cause, yet understanding self-injury in this way can enrich our work greatly.

Authoritarian approaches

It is very tempting to respond to the concern which self-injury causes to us and to the responsibilities and expectations placed on us by simply forbidding it. We tell the person she may not self-injure while on our ward/ in our hostel / attending our group / in therapy. Perhaps we get her to sign a contract. Or she is put on supervision, with staff at the ready to prevent her from hurting herself.

Unfortunately, while such strategies seem to get rid of the problem, in fact they may well compound it. Few people with any spirit respond well to being forbidden to do things which are important to them. They resent it. They start to look for ways round it. Many people say that when they have been forbidden to self-injure they have begun to hide and lie about their injuries. When prevented from hurting themselves they have 'made up for lost time' with even more self-injury as soon as they got the chance. (Meanwhile the workers involved presumably think their strategy has worked.)

Of course there are some situations in which statutory responsibility may compel workers to try to prevent someone from harming themselves seriously. But generally an authoritarian approach is unnecessary and interferes with our ability to build up good, honest, helping relationships with the people we work with. This issue and other ways of proceeding will be explored more fully in Chapter 5.

Rescuing

Another very human and indeed caring response to our anxiety and distress about self-injury is to want to rescue the person. We cannot bear what they are doing to themselves, and we are sure we can stop them, if we can only provide enough support and caring.

"I feel like I'll do anything to help her not to cut. I've told her she can ring me any time and talk instead. I know I shouldn't react like this, but I feel so hurt and let down when she does it anyway."

Of course it is important to care and to provide support. But for our own sakes (and our clients') we have to set reasonable limits on what we offer. We cannot protect anyone else from their own pain. They have to bear it and find new ways of coping with it in their own way, and in their own time. Hopefully we can be a valuable resource for them in this process, but to do so we have to let them take responsibility for themselves. Our reward can be to know we have helped someone to truly grow. What **we** may need help to bear is our own anxiety and powerlessness.

Fortunately, there are many things we can do to help us avoid the sorts of pitfalls described above, and to work confidently and effectively. The rest of this handbook is concerned with these things.

Chapter 3
Why do people self-injure?

Put at its simplest, people self-injure because it makes them feel better for a time, and helps them to cope.

Research into the backgrounds of people who injure themselves has found that most have suffered (and sometimes continue to endure) extremely traumatic or stressful life experiences and circumstances. Without opportunities to express and receive support for these distressing experiences, their emotional pain comes to feel unbearable. Injuring their own bodies serves their desperate need to somehow survive this pain. The ways in which it can do this - the functions, meanings or purposes of self-injury - are complex and need to be explored further. First we look in more detail at the sorts of experiences which tend to underlie self-injury.

Life experiences which may underlie self-injury

The experiences which people who self-injure report as causing their distress often occur in childhood. For many, a difficult childhood is followed by further painful experiences in adult life, which reinforce their need to cope in this way.

Childhood experiences found to underlie self-injury include:

Sexual, physical and/or emotional abuse

Neglect and deprivation (physical and emotional)

Loss of a parent (through death or separation)

Parental illness or alcoholism

Severe lack of communication in the home (particularly about feelings, problems and needs)

Chronic childhood illness or disability

Being subjected to excessively high expectations

Bullying and rejection by peers

Racial harassment and oppression

Fear and shame about sexuality

Of these the first two categories - abuse and neglect of various kinds - are the most commonly reported. Many people mention having suffered as a result of several of the experiences listed.

As we know, such experiences in childhood often leave people carrying a burden of extreme unhappiness and distress. They also interfere with development. The person may not have the chance to develop the internal strengths and resources they need to cope with life and relationships as adults. Particularly if there has been little support and communication, they may not learn how to manage and articulate their own feelings. These factors can all play a part in leading someone to self-injure.

For many people, further painful experiences follow in adult life. Some people do not attribute their self-injury to childhood experiences at all, but begin to hurt themselves following a trauma in adult life. Experiences in adult life which people report as leading to self-injury are strikingly similar to those significant in childhood.

Such experiences include:

Rape and abusive sexual experiences

Abusive partner (physically and/or emotionally)

Lack of support / communication

Loss of a child or infertility

Loss of a partner (death or relationship breakdown)

Incarceration in prison or psychiatric hospital

Own serious illness.

Again the themes of abuse and loss are important, as are lack of communication and emotional support. Incarceration in prison or hospital has its parallel for children in being placed in Care or prolonged hospitalisation, (and for some, placement in boarding school).

The effects of such experiences often include severe, on-going emotional pain. Many people who self-injure report that their lives are dominated by overwhelming feelings of sadness, grief, desperation, depression or hopelessness. They may also have been left with very low self-esteem and a sense of self-blame. Often self-injury is carried out in order to deal with feelings of self-hatred, guilt, shame, 'dirtiness' or 'badness'.

People may also carry a legacy of anger, frustration or a sense of powerlessness which can lead to their impulses to hurt themselves. These feelings arise in response to being badly treated, ignored or controlled by others, and being unable to protest or to take action to change their situation.

Experiences of abuse, neglect and so on can also result in unbearable anxiety, panic, fear or tension, which can drive people to seek release through self-injury.

Emotional deprivation and isolation in childhood often leave people feeling very needy, yet unable to express their needs, nor to provide care, compassion and nurturing for themselves. In adult life they may also be unsupported or unheard by others. Self-injury can sometimes be a response to their feelings of neediness and isolation.

Some people cope with traumatic experiences by numbing themselves. They come to feel dead or unreal, which though it anaesthetises pain, can be terrifying. These feelings may also precipitate self-injury.

It is extremely helpful for those working and supporting people who self-injure to be aware of the range and nature of feelings which may give rise to self-injury. It enables us to understand better, and to show the person we are working with that it is possible for their self-injury to be understood. We are able to respond more appropriately, acknowledging the person's deep feelings of distress, rather than focusing solely on the physical injury. And we can help the person to explore and verbalise their own emotions - something they may never have learned to do in their lives.

Functions served by self-injury

From talking with many people who self-injure it is clear that, however negative and self-destructive it may be to hurt one's own body, it also serves many important functions. Self-injury is primarily a way to cope, to feel better, to bear what might otherwise be unbearable. In some cases it may feel like the only way to deal with feelings so distressing that the alternative is suicide.

"It is better to have a few more scars than to be dead"

How, exactly, does hurting themselves help a person to cope? Self-injury can serve a whole range of functions.

Relief of feelings

One of the most important ways in which self-injury helps people to cope is as a way of relieving unbearable emotional distress.

"Sometimes it's a way of showing myself just how awful I feel. Other times I just do it, cover it up and forget about it - it helps me get rid of what I'm feeling so I can get on with 'coping' in the world."

We all have the need to express our feelings. For some people self-injury may feel like the only way of doing this. (This is particularly likely to be the case if someone has not been allowed to show her feelings, and has been subjected to criticism or abuse if she did so.) The wound on the body symbolically shows the terrible psychic wounds the person feels. Through hurting themselves someone may be able to release feelings which feel unbearable when held inside.

Sometimes emotions are experienced only as enormous tension. People who have not been helped as children (or adults) to name their feelings may not be able to identify quite what it is they feel. Or the tension may be the result of desperately trying to suppress feelings which seem terrifying or unjustified. Many people describe a feeling of intolerable pressure inside.

"It's like a volcano building up inside me, getting hotter and hotter. I have to cut myself to let some of it out or I'd just explode."

This release may be followed by words or tears, as the person finally allows their emotions through.

For some people it seems very important to see a tangible wound on the outside of the body. This helps them to translate invisible, inner pain into something they can see and deal with. What felt unmanageable has become manageable. At the same time the wound can serve as 'evidence' that they are really hurt - there is a 'real' reason for their distress. We can see how important this may feel to someone who has been told that there is nothing wrong and they have no justification for their feelings.

"I was always told that I shouldn't make such a big fuss about nothing. I say it to myself now. It's hard when I'm upset to know whether it's justified, or I'm just being silly. If I see a wound on myself, it's like it proves there really is something wrong".

Another way in which self-injury can help someone cope is by providing distraction. Physical pain and injury take the focus away from what feels like worse emotional pain. Sometimes it leaves the person feeling quite numb - giving some respite from their internal torment.

It will be clear that the ways in which self-injury may help someone relieve unbearable feelings can be very varied and complex. This can give us some clues when working to help someone deal with their feelings in other ways. If the primary function of their self-injury, for example, is to release tension caused by the suppression of feelings, they may benefit from help in learning how to express their emotions safely. If a person's feelings are all too vivid and overwhelming, they may prefer to explore other ways to contain them, or to comfort and support themselves in coping with them.

Self-punishment and atonement

Most, if not all people who self-injure carry feelings of self-hatred and self-blame, and a belief that they are bad, evil, dirty or contaminated. Of course, most of us experience some of these sorts of feelings at times, and we can be hard on ourselves as a result. When such feelings are very powerful, people may self-injure in order to punish themselves, and so earn some respite from their feelings. For a while they can feel that, through their pain and injury, they have 'atoned' for what they see as their wrongdoing or badness. Guilt and self-loathing are terrible burdens, and it can be a tremendous relief to feel one has 'paid for' one's crimes.

For people who see themselves as dirty (often as a result of abuse), self-injury may also be a way of symbolically ridding themselves of the contamination they feel.

"When it bleeds I feel like some of the dirt and badness are coming out of me. I can then feel clean for a while."

However self-destructive such actions are, the impetus behind them can again be positive. The person wants to feel better, to free themselves of their self-hatred, to rid themselves of what feels wrong or alien inside. Unfortunately, such feelings of self-forgiveness and cleansing tend to be quite short-lived. Until the reasons for the person's self-blame and loathing are properly resolved the feelings will build up again, demanding more self-punishment.

Replaying abusive experiences

Self-punishment may also bring relief by recreating what is familiar. For someone who has been abused, punishment is what is known, painful but somehow feeling 'safe'. Perhaps when they were a child incidents of violence or abuse were followed by affection, or by periods of relative stability. Being punished came to feel like the one way in which things could be made 'all right' again. In adult life, feelings of anxiety, neediness or sadness might lead the person to seek the same 'solution' through punishing themselves. The replaying of punishment and abuse may also be carried out in an attempt to remember, deal with and resolve one's past experiences.

Control

For many people, self-injury provides a way of feeling they have control over at least something in their lives.

We all need to feel that we have a reasonable degree of control over what happens to us, and that we can speak and act to affect our situation. Most people who self-injure, however, have been (and may continue to be) made very powerless. Perhaps other people in their lives have exercised great (and often abusive) power over them. Or life events such as illness or bereavement have left them feeling they have no control over what happens to them.

They can, however, control the injuries to their own bodies, determining the nature, site, timing and severity of their wounds. Perhaps there is satisfaction in being able to hurt oneself before others do, or to inflict and endure worse injuries than someone else can. Self-injury may also be a way of 'staking claim' to one's own body.

Some people also feel that by injuring themselves they can control feelings of anger, which they fear might otherwise lead them to hurt someone else. (They may not actually be at risk of hurting someone else. Often it is more that the power of their anger feels 'murderous'.)

Clearly, where a person's only means of achieving a sense of control or agency in their lives is through self-injury, others' attempts to stop them from hurting themselves are likely to be counter-productive. We can imagine how terrifying and infuriating it would be to have what feels like our last vestige of control taken away from us. If we had any spirit left, we would fight or lie to hold on to this. Understanding this can help workers to feel less perplexed and frustrated by a person's determination to hold on to self-injury, despite all their efforts to help them.

Communication

For most people, self-injury serves many internal functions - it is carried out primarily to regulate their own feelings, rather than in order to gain a response from others. Some people in fact never show or tell anyone else about their injuries. However, self-injury can also be a way of trying to communicate something, but without words.

When people try to communicate their distress through self-injury, it is because their experiences have taught them that they have no right or that it is not safe to communicate verbally. They have had no reason to believe that they will be taken seriously if they speak about their experiences, needs and feelings.

The 'message' may be that something terribly wrong is happening in their lives, or that they are in great pain. The person's wounds may 'speak' for them of their anger and protest, as well as of their neediness and despair.

A person may also create injuries upon their body to reflect the ugliness and messiness they feel inside themselves. Perhaps this is a way of trying to drive others away, perhaps it is to test whether they can be accepted and cared for even when their 'true' selves are known. It may be both - people who self-injure can feel very ambivalent about seeking contact with others. They long for recognition and support, yet are terrified of exposing their vulnerability, shame and neediness (justifiably, given their experiences). This may be one reason why people sometimes half-conceal their injuries. Their wounds are hidden yet some hint of them is given away.

It is important that as workers we receive the communication which comes to us via self-injury, but that we remember to tread gently and respectfully. We should not shame, frighten or intrude upon a person who is reaching out in this way.

Comfort and nurturing

"It's like it's a reason to look after myself and love myself. I feel I don't deserve it the rest of the time. It's my secret comfort, that no-one can take away from me."

Perhaps surprisingly, self-injury can be experienced as calming or comforting. This can come not only from the release of tension, but from the satisfaction in having something 'special' that one can do for oneself. Sometimes an injury serves to provide a rare opportunity for nurture; perhaps the only time when a person feels deserving of care. Often people tend their injuries themselves, but sometimes the wound provides an 'excuse' to seek help from others.

It can be very frustrating for workers (for example in Accident and Emergency departments) to be repeatedly faced with someone who has hurt themselves seemingly 'for attention'. Professionals and supporters may try desperately to convince someone that it is not necessary for them to hurt themselves in order to receive care or comfort. Sometimes they react to their frustration by deciding to ignore the person's self-injury, and to give attention only when the person does not hurt themselves.

The feelings behind such a policy are understandable but the practice is in fact cruel and unhelpful. A person who comforts herself or looks for caring through self-injury does so because she has already been severely deprived of these things in her life. She has probably had few examples of loving comfort from which to learn how to soothe herself. She has been taught that it is pointless or dangerous to ask for what she needs. Given such experiences, it is positive that the person can comfort themselves or ask for nurturing in **any** way. This can give them (and us) something to build on in finding less harmful ways. But change is bound to take considerable time, practice and patience.

Making one's body unattractive

"Nobody's going to bother me now, with all these scars."

Sometimes women injure themselves to make their bodies unattractive in the hope this will keep away others whom they fear, particularly someone who abuses them sexually.

Feeling real or alive

Sometimes people self-injure as a way to prove to themselves that they are alive, real or human. They do this because their experiences in life have left them feeling numb, 'dead' or unreal.

'Switching off' can be a good survival strategy for someone whose life is full of pain which they cannot do anything about (such as a child who is repeatedly abused). But this can leave someone feeling trapped and isolated in frightening numbness or detachment. Hurting one's body can break through these feelings.

"A lot of the time I feel unreal and not part of the world everyone else belongs in. When I hurt myself I feel like I'm here and in touch."

Discussion

When we begin to look at some of the functions self-injury can fulfil, we realise that people often hurt themselves to achieve surprisingly positive ends. It is positive to want to feel better and to cope, to have ways of feeling safe and comforted, to rid oneself of guilt and contamination. It is healthy to want to communicate, to protest, to try to gain control of one's life, and so on. A person who self-injures for such reasons wants to survive and to make things better for themselves. This is a fundamentally healthy urge, and it can provide a basis on which to work with someone towards less harmful ways of dealing with life.

It is very important for us as workers to recognise how essential self-injury may be to a person's ability to cope. This will alert us to the futility, or even danger, of attempting to simply stop someone from hurting themselves, before they have developed other coping strategies. It can reassure us that we are right not to interfere. Instead we can begin to explore with the person what support they need to make self-injury less essential to their survival.

Chapter 4
How can we help?

There are many ways in which any worker who comes into contact with people who self-injure can be helpful.

Of course, the precise nature and extent of the help that we can offer depends upon our role. A nurse working in an Accident and Emergency Department offers different things from a helpline worker. A social worker has a very different role from a teacher, and so on. Nevertheless, there are many similarities in the ways each can help. In this chapter we look first at some fundamental principles which are helpful in any contact with someone who self-injures. We go on to consider what can be offered in longer-term work.

The basics

Helping someone to raise the subject of self-injury

It is very rare for people to feel safe and comfortable about telling someone they self-injure. Most people feel ashamed and embarrassed. They know others are likely to be shocked and perhaps to condemn them, to misunderstand or to try to take control over them. They may feel that exposing their self-injury also shows their emotional pain and vulnerability. People may therefore hide or lie about their injuries. If they do tell they may appear blasé or even aggressive, but this usually masks fear and shame. Even in situations where their self-injury is not a secret, they may be very reluctant to discuss the subject.

There are a number of ways in which workers can make it easier for the topic of self-injury to be broached:

Literature: Having leaflets, posters or books around which deal with the topic of self-injury can let people know that this is a topic they can discuss. (Some books are suggested in the References and Resources section on page 75. Projects can also write their own information sheets about self-injury.) If appropriate, information about the services being offered can mention self-injury at some point, so that people know it is 'on the agenda'.

Being aware of self-injury: The more alert workers are to the possibility that someone may self-injure, the more likely they are to be able to pick up clues and hints that the person may drop. The knowledge that someone has undergone some of the sorts of experiences listed in Chapter 3 may suggest that self-injury (or some other sort of self-harm) could be an issue for them. Particular clues to self-injury include frequent 'accidents', wearing long sleeves in hot weather, and references to being afraid of what one might do, or to having 'done something silly'.

Providing opportunities to talk: We can make it easier for people to raise the topic of self-injury by being available and approachable. There needs to be privacy, and we should try to provide the opportunity for people to speak to someone with whom they are likely to feel safe (e.g. of the same sex).

We encourage disclosure of difficult topics such as self-injury by listening and responding non-judgmentally to other things people talk about. We can also invite the topic ourselves, if we feel it is relevant. It is less threatening to do this indirectly, by making a statement such as "sometimes people who have been through difficult experiences like yours do things to hurt themselves", rather than by asking a direct question.

Responding to disclosures about self-injury

When someone does begin to talk about their self-injury, we offer something truly valuable (and rare) if we respond with acceptance and kindness. Exactly what needs to be said will vary, but here are some suggestions for things which will help form the basis of helpful responses:

1. **Acceptance**
   Make it clear that it is okay to talk about self-injury. It is something which you know about and can handle.

2. **Acknowledgement**
   Acknowledge how hard it can be to talk about self-injury, and the courage it takes to do so.

3. **Concern**
   Show your concern for the distress which lies behind the person's self-injury.

4. **Understanding**
   Make it clear that self-injury is something which can be understood, that there are reasons for it and that it is something many other people who have had difficult experiences do too.

5. **Respect and reassurance**
   Acknowledge that self-injury has been an important means of survival for the person. Reassure them that you understand how frightening it can be to contemplate living without self-injury, and that you will not try to take away their coping strategy from them.

6. **Hope**
   People may believe that they are trapped in hurting themselves, and will never be able to stop. Reassure them that it is possible to stop, that many other people have, but that it's okay to do this at their own pace.

7. **Information**
   Provide information about appropriate resources, such as counselling or support services, as well as literature. But don't rush to send the person elsewhere, or they may feel 'fobbed off', or that they are too much for anyone to cope with. Remember that you are offering something real and valuable right now, by being there and listening.

8. **Confidentiality**
   Respect confidentiality. Don't panic and rush to tell others (e.g. doctor or family) about a person's self-injury. Remember that they have probably been hurting themselves in private for some time, and they are still alive. Breaking confidentiality can destroy trust and make the person likely to be secretive and wary of seeking help.

   You may have agency policies which require that you report something like self-injury to a manager or other professional. If this is so, you can safeguard trust by letting the person know early on in the conversation that you may not be able to keep confidentiality, so that they can decide whether to talk further.

   If you simply feel that someone else could help the person further, you could suggest this. Support them in telling others themselves in their own time, so that they continue to feel in control of the information others have about them.

9. **Gentle enquiry**
   It may be appropriate (depending on the individual worker's role, time available, etc.) to invite the person to talk about some of the feelings and experiences which lie behind their self-injury. It is important not to probe into a person's background if you cannot offer enough time and support for disclosures which may make them upset and vulnerable. On the other hand, many people are desperate for someone to ask them **why** they hurt themselves (and to listen and care about the answer).

10. Responding to injuries

If there are recent injuries, show concern for these too. Someone who has just hurt themselves is usually upset and vulnerable (although they may hide this). The fact that they have caused the wound themselves does not mean it will not hurt, or be frightening and shocking to them. Concern for them gives them a message that they matter and deserve care, which will almost certainly be something they have had far too little of in their lives.

If you think the person's injuries need medical attention and you are not in a position to give this, gently suggest that they go to someone who can treat the injuries. But usually there is no rush - you can take time to talk first. And nobody should be forced to go to hospital if they don't want to. Often people are reluctant to seek medical help because of bad experiences. It may be possible for you to offer to go along with them as a supporter and advocate, or to discuss who else might fulfil this role.

Professionals and supporters often fear that showing sympathy will 'reinforce' the person's self-injury, and they may think they should give minimal attention or show disapproval. In our experience a withholding or punitive attitude can make a person feel even worse about themselves, and so even more likely to self-injure. Even if someone does self-injure partly as a means of 'deserving' care, this need not be a problem. At least they are acknowledging their need for caring, and in the longer-term they can work on developing ways of getting this without hurting themselves. For the moment, they are doing the best they can.

What about your own feelings?

Being told about someone's self-injury for the first time is likely to bring up some of the feelings discussed in Chapter One: shock, fear, disgust, sadness, and so on. People often fear that they will betray such feelings, and 'say the wrong thing' at this point.

It is not wrong to be human, and to show that you are upset or worried about someone's self-injury. In fact, it may help the person to see that you are concerned. The most important thing is to take responsibility for your own feelings. What *is* wrong and unhelpful is to blame the person for upsetting you. There is a world of difference, for example, between saying:

"I'm worried about your injuries and I feel a bit out of my depth. Perhaps we should think about getting someone to look at them?" and:

"Roll your sleeve down! I don't know how you could do something so sick and horrible!".

Similarly, it is very different for the person to hear you say:

"I feel really sad that you have felt so desperate that you needed to hurt yourself." rather than:

"You've upset me so much, after I've tried to help you."

Of course if we are in a helping role with someone, the real place for our own distress is somewhere else, with our own peers or supervisors and managers. (This will be discussed further in Chapter 6.)

On-going work

Some workers only have one-off or intermittent contact with someone who self-injures. Others are in a role which involves on-going contact and support of various kinds. Below we explore a range of ways in which workers in many different roles can help people who self-injure. (Detailed suggestions for therapy with people who self-injure are given in the book 'The Language of Injury' by Lois Arnold and Gloria Babiker, see References, page 75).

In many ways what is helpful to people who self-injure is no different from the things which would be helpful to anyone else who was suffering distress following painful life experiences. Long-term treatment for self-injury is not specific (except perhaps where cognitive or behavioural approaches are used). The skills and empathy that we would offer others we were helping and supporting are just as relevant to people who self-injure. Much of what is suggested below, therefore, is not specific only to self-injury. The particular application to self-injury is, however, discussed. Some specific suggestions for approaches focusing on self-injury are also included.

Relationships

Relationships with workers

Workers in many different roles who are involved on an on-going basis with someone who self-injures can offer the person the opportunity to experience positive, respectful relationships.

From our knowledge of the backgrounds of people who self-injure it is clear that many will not have experienced much in the way of good, caring relationships in the past. The adults who were responsible for their nurturing and protection as children may have been abusive, absent, or unable to meet their needs. As adults those with power in their lives (sometimes including other professionals) may have been dismissive, uncaring or abusive. Opportunities for communicating and receiving support for feelings and problems are likely to have been very limited.

An on-going relationship with a worker can be an opportunity for an individual to begin to redress their negative experience. If the person can experience a reasonable degree of consistency, caring, acceptance, respect and healthy boundaries they can gradually begin to learn that relationships with others can be safe and fulfilling. Over time they will also internalise some of the respect and caring they receive. Gradually the power of negative 'messages' and beliefs from the past will be reduced, while more positive foundations will be laid down.

This process is bound to take time - the individual is 'unlearning' years of negative experience of relationships. They may be very afraid to trust and to believe things can be different. It may take a long time before the foundations laid down by a caring relationship are manifested in obvious change in a person's life and behaviour. A relationship with one worker may be only one (albeit valuable) step on a person's longer journey, whose end the worker may unfortunately never see. Workers need to recognise this and hold on to the knowledge that what they are doing by continuing to be alongside a person in a caring, respectful way really is of value.

"Looking back, I can remember people from years ago who were great and really made a difference to me. They probably never saw it - I was too busy telling them to get lost. But I think that the fact that they did bother and cared about me showed me that it was possible, and that I could get help. Those people still shine out in my mind, all these years later."

Relationships with peers

Positive and helpful relationships with non-professionals are also very important. There can be elements of sharing, mutual responsibility, equality and friendship with peers which are not possible in a relationship with a professional.

In services where clients come into contact with each other naturally (such as residential services, schools, day hospitals, prisons, drop-in centres, etc.) workers can encourage the development of supportive relationships between users of the services. Structured opportunities such as support groups or shared activities can help.

It is just as important to foster a general atmosphere of respect and support for one another within the project. This requires that staff themselves respect and support users, seeing them as people with strengths and resources as well as difficulties. Where people are infantilised, treated disrespectfully and offered too little support they may become competitive and manipulative. They are unlikely to be able to offer much to others. (If service users do identify with each other in such a context it may be in opposition to staff and rebellion against the regime. Whilst this is in fact quite a healthy response, it is quite likely to foster self-injury and other sorts of self-harm.) Individuals are most likely to be able to build relationships and support each other where they feel empowered by choice, respect and support for their own development.

In services where users do not normally come into contact with each other, such as those offering individual counselling, workers could consider setting up or referring clients to peer support groups. Many people who self-injure find these extremely helpful. Groups focusing on issues such as the effects of childhood abuse may be appropriate and helpful. Groups specifically for people who self-injure are very rare and are greatly needed. Professionals often seem wary of such groups, fearing that they will somehow encourage the self-injury. In an adequately supported group, however, the opposite is true. Group members can provide each other with acceptance, support, ideas and sometimes challenging which are very valuable in helping each other to move forward.

Communication and self-expression

Communication is of course an essential aspect of relationships and will develop naturally as a helping relationship continues. However, communication merits particular attention in work with people who self-injure. It was seen earlier that often such people have not been allowed in childhood (or later) to express themselves in words, tears and so on. Self-injury has become a way in which they 'speak' of their pain. They may have particular difficulty in verbalising (or even identifying) their experiences, feelings and needs, and can benefit from help in translating these into words or other means of expression.

We can help people to communicate about the things which underlie their self-injury in a number of ways:

1. Making it clear we are willing to hear about their experiences, feelings and needs, that we can bear to stay alongside and will support them in their distress.

2. Helping the person to identify and name their feelings by supportively suggesting possibilities, e.g. *"You must have been in an awful lot of pain to need to hurt yourself like that"; "I expect you must have felt really sad about that?"; "I imagine that experience would be very frightening?"*. You may get it wrong but you have brought feelings onto the agenda and shown that you will empathise with these. By considering what you have suggested and deciding whether it fits, refining it, and so on, the person can gradually develop their own awareness and emotional vocabulary.

3. Being patient and not pushing: recognising that it may be terrifying for the person to experience and articulate any feeling, and that to do so is a big step forward.

4. Offering and responding to different modes of communication and expression.

Many people for whom it is hard to verbalise feelings do, however, find it helpful to write. Drawing, painting, clay, etc. are also very valuable ways of exploring and conveying experiences, which people who self-injure often take to and enjoy. It can also be helpful for someone to express themselves physically, for example by running, exercise at a gym, or by punching something (soft), smashing things, and so on. People may also feel that someone else's expression through music or poetry can 'speak' for them.

As workers we can help people gain access to materials and facilities, and by attending and responding to what has been written, drawn or expressed in some way.

Looking at underlying issues

Most people who self-injure say that what has really helped or would help them is an opportunity to explore and resolve the issues which underlie their self-injury. These may include both current and past experiences and life circumstances. Often this will involve dealing with very painful material concerning abuse, loss or other trauma. It is therefore not something to be undertaken lightly.

The precise ways in which we as individual workers can help with this depends upon our role, our skills and experience and the time we can offer. We may need to refer the person to someone else who has the time and experience to work with very powerful material which will take a long time to resolve. We can all help by acknowledging to a person who harms themselves that there **are** good reasons for what they do and by providing information on services available to help them deal with their experiences.

Where a professional undertakes to work with someone on underlying experiences, the self-injury can provide important clues to material which needs attention. This point will be explored further below (pages 44-46).

Practical help

A person might need practical help as well as opportunities to talk. The sorts of practical problems which may contribute to a person's drive to self-injure include: lack of money, poor accommodation, violence or harassment, isolation, unemployment or unsatisfactory working conditions, lack of support for their role as a parent or carer, illness, difficulties with school or college work, and so on. Obtaining help with such problems can make a very real difference. If we can't help directly ourselves, we can offer accurate information about other agencies which can do so.

Support

Most people who self-injure have a great need for support. Some find it hard to acknowledge their need and to accept support. Others may make great use of services and their needs can sometimes seem endless and insatiable.

Everyone needs support from others in their lives, especially when they are feeling low, or have practical difficulties. People need others to recognise their need for support, to listen to them and take them seriously. They need others to empathise with their feelings and to care about them. These are the things which people who self-injure also need, sometimes urgently and in large amounts.

Most people are also able to support themselves to a reasonable extent - they have inner resources on which they can call in order to cope and comfort themselves when times are hard. If they received at least a reasonable amount of love, comfort and empathy as children, they are able to develop their own resources and ways of meeting their own needs. They build things into their lives which support them: friends, activities they enjoy, 'treats', places they go, and so on. We all need others, but we can cope on our own most of the time.

Children who do not receive enough love and support do not have the opportunity to build up a 'store' of care for themselves, nor to learn how to soothe themselves. If others have not empathised and supported them in bearing upsetting feelings, they will not have learned how to cope with and contain their own distress. (Hence, for some, self-injury.) This means that as adults they may need more support, at least for a while, than most people can manage with. They need some of the caring which was lacking in childhood, to help them to bear their feelings and difficulties while they build up their own resources. This need may increase when a person is exploring experiences underlying their self-injury, and is trying to change and give up this way of coping.

Working with people who find it hard to accept support

Some people who self-injure find it very difficult to ask for support, or to accept and let it in when it is offered. They may believe that it is not okay for them to have needs at all, or that, if unleashed, their needs would be overwhelming. They may prefer to do anything rather than become aware of the terrible pain of their unmet childhood needs. And the prospect of asking anyone else for support brings with it the fear of vulnerability, rejection, hurt and shame. Such people may self-injure in response to any feelings of emotional need, or may even hurt themselves after someone has listened and supported them, because they feel so guilty and undeserving. This can be hard for caring workers who want to offer support. It is frustrating if someone persists in not trusting us or making use of what we want to offer, perhaps going off alone to hurt themselves when they could be drawing support from us. We need great patience to carry on being there while the person gradually learns that someone really does want to know.

We can help the person by conveying that we understand how frightening it can be to trust and allow someone to help. They have had good reason to be scared. We can take care not to be intrusive, and to respectfully back off (while remaining available) when someone needs to keep their distance. Developing trust in this way can be seen as work which is in itself very important and valuable, rather than just being a preparation for the 'real work' of counselling or therapy.

Working with people who demand a lot of support

In contrast to people who do not easily admit their need, there are people who demand a great deal of support. Sometimes they are in contact with many workers in a number of services, yet it seems as if, however much support they are offered, it is never enough. To workers such people can feel overwhelming, their needs insatiable. The person themselves may feel similarly overwhelmed and terrified by their own neediness.

It is very easy for caring yet overstretched workers to become frustrated with people such as this, to begin avoiding them, and to see them as unreasonable and a nuisance. This is understandable, but it is important to pull back from such feelings and try to understand what is going on for the person when they make such seemingly endless demands. It can help if we try to imagine how it must feel to be so needy, and so lacking in resources to bear such needy feelings. It must be terrifying not to know how to even begin meeting your own emotional needs. Often the person will have had a life largely devoid of true caring and empathy, and will have very little self-esteem or respect for themselves. Perhaps they have been in 'the System' for years, which is likely to have made them see themselves as sick, inadequate and unable to make choices and take responsibility for themselves.

Of course no individual worker or even team of workers can fulfil all of a person's support needs. The limits on what support can be offered will vary according to the circumstances and personalities involved. Some helpful guidelines on supporting people who self-injure are:

1. Communicate that it is okay for the person to need and ask for support, even if you are not always able to provide it. It is not wrong or shameful to need support from others.

2. Ask the person what sorts of support they need, when, under what conditions, and so on.

3. Work out for yourself, with your client and perhaps in consultation with colleagues or a supervisor, how you can respond to the person's needs. It is helpful if you are in a position to be flexible in offering support, for example more frequent contact at times of greater need. However, it is vital to be clear with yourself and your client about your own limits. Take care not to offer more than you can actually give without becoming burnt out or resentful. It is far better to offer what you genuinely can manage than to commit yourself to something you cannot later fulfil. For example, you may feel you could offer a couple of 'ring-in times' per week, when the person may call if they need to, but you do not want to be telephoned at all hours.

4. Collect information to make available to clients about other resources available in the area, including voluntary sector and self-help facilities, helplines, etc.

5. Encourage the person to explore ways of gradually developing their own support. This may involve helping them to identify and build up things in their lives which will contribute to their strength and well-being. They may also need help to recognise and deal with aspects of their lives which diminish their ability to cope.

Focusing on the self-injury

Sometimes it may be appropriate or important for work with someone who hurts themselves to specifically focus on the self-injury. There are several reasons for this:

- Self-injury may be an important part of the person's daily life, about which they have complex and ambivalent feelings, which needs to be brought into the work.

- Self-injury is a means of expression as well as of coping. By regularly talking about the self-injury and the feelings and circumstances which give rise to it, a person can learn to translate their experiences into words, rather than acting them out through harming themselves.

- Incidents of self-injury may be coded signals of difficulties in a person's past or current life with which they need help.

- Where there is an on-going relationship between a worker and client, self-injury may sometimes relate to issues between them. The client may feel angry, unheard, or let down by the worker. This needs to be brought out into the open and communicated directly to resolve the issue.

- The person may want help in finding ways to stop or reduce their self-injury.

- The worker may feel concerned for the client's safety and see it as part of their professional responsibility to try to help them reduce the harm they do to themselves.

Earlier (pages 31-33) we listed a number of principles which can guide workers in responding helpfully to someone who discloses self-injury. Many of these will also be relevant when discussing self-injury with someone in the context of on-going work. Acceptance, caring and respect are fundamental, and will themselves help ease some of the shame, secrecy, isolation and low self-esteem which can feed self-injury. In longer-term work, however, further possibilities may be available:

Building understanding

Workers can explore with clients the feelings and situations (past and present) which seem to precipitate incidents of self-injury, such as feeling upset, angry or unheard, being overburdened or isolated, and so on. It is important to note that self-injury may reflect current as well as past life circumstances and difficulties. Where this emerges, it is clearly important that the situation itself is tackled, as well as the self-injury.

"We had a patient who kept on cutting herself, whatever we did. It turned out she was being abused by another worker. Once that stopped, so did the cutting."

By also exploring how the person feels *after* hurting herself, it is possible to build up an understanding of the particular functions self-injury fulfils for her. It is likely that there will be a number of these functions. The same person may sometimes hurt herself in order to relieve unbearable distress or anger, at other times to feel she has some control in her life, sometimes to communicate her desperation to others, and so on.

Such understanding can lead to acknowledgement of the person's reasons for self-injury and their resourcefulness in finding a way to cope. It also paves the way for exploration of alternative, less harmful means of fulfilling the same functions.

Self-injury is of course also destructive and hateful to oneself. What are probably justified feelings of anger and hatred are being visited upon the self, instead of being directed outside at those who have caused the original hurts. It is important that this is also acknowledged in working with people who hurt themselves. We can help them to acknowledge the part of themselves which wants to cause the harm, while supporting the part which can be more self-nurturing and protective.

Extending choice

"In groups we help people to share different ways they cope and express themselves"

Once someone understands something about the ways in which self-injury functions for her, she can begin to explore other choices for herself. If, for example, she is hurting herself to contain her feelings about an intolerable relationship or job, she might be able to begin acknowledging how unhappy she feels and to think about ways of changing her situation. If she self-injures to cope with her feelings of grief, helplessness and anger about abuse or loss in her past, she may be able to share her feelings in words and tears.

In the long run, this is how self-injury stops: the need for it falls away as the person resolves issues in her life and becomes more able to bear and express her feelings and needs. However, this usually takes considerable time and support.

Reducing harm

Whilst a person is still injuring themselves it may be possible to help them to keep themselves safer and to reduce the degree of harm they do. This is reassuring to both workers and clients. Most people who self-injure feel ambivalent if not frightened about the risk and damage they cause themselves, and can feel relieved and empowered if they are able to set some limits on this.

Workers can help by:

- supportively helping the person to learn about risks, how to self-injure more 'safely' and how to take care of their injuries

- exploring with the person the limits they would like to set on their own self-injury. For example, someone may feel she wants to continue cutting but not burning, or that she would like to avoid cutting so deep as to require suturing. Discussion can then focus on support or strategies which would help her stick to these limits.

- helping them to identify times when they are most at risk - such as when tired, after drinking, when alone, after an argument - and to develop strategies for avoiding or coping with such situations and triggers.

Giving up self-injury

Often a person will say that they want to give up injuring themselves. Here workers can help by:

1. Discussing with them how ready they are to cope without self-injury and what might be the difficulties. It is also essential for the person to acknowledge their ambivalence and the part of them that may want to carry on hurting themselves, as well as the part that wants to stop.

2. Exploring workable approaches. It is often far more realistic to take a step-by-step approach, setting small, realistic goals. These could involve such things as slightly reducing the severity, frequency and/or extent of the injuries, bit by bit, or trying to go for a manageable trial period (a day, a week, etc.) without self-injury and then reviewing how this felt.

3. Acknowledging the courage and strength involved in achieving each small step. Where the person does not manage to stick to their plan, it is important to offer

reassurance and encouragement and to use the situation as an opportunity to learn and review things. Perhaps the goal was unrealistic, perhaps there were particular stresses or triggers which need to be dealt with, etc.

4. Giving extra support where needed (or helping the person gain access to increased support from other sources, such as a self-help group, telephone helpline, etc.)

5. Helping the client explore and plan strategies and alternatives for crisis moments (see *Exploring alternatives*, below).

6. Helping the person acknowledge the loss involved in giving up self-injury. As one woman said: *"When I stopped cutting I felt like I'd lost my best friend and my worst enemy".*

Exploring alternatives

People who self-injure frequently try to avoid hurting themselves at times of crisis or distress. It can help enormously for them to have a repertoire of alternative ways of coping on which they can call at such times. Those trying to give up self-injury also find this very valuable. Workers can help individuals explore and try out alternatives to self-injury, identifying those which work for them, and under what circumstances.

Some alternatives which people who self-injure have themselves suggested as helpful include:

Expressing feelings and difficulties:

talking (face to face or telephone)
writing (letters, odd words, poems, stories)
drawing/painting, photography, clay, music
punching or kicking (something soft)
dance and movement
shouting, screaming, crying

48

Relaxation:

warm bath
aromatherapy
yoga
massage (by self or other person)
relaxation tapes, music

Exercise:

walking, running
cycling, swimming
gym, weights
dance and movement

Nurturing:

physical comfort from someone else
self-nurture, e.g. creating a warm 'sanctuary' at home, putting oneself to bed with a hot drink, treating oneself as one would a distressed child

Self-esteem / dealing with self-hatred:

writing down good things about oneself
use of affirmations (written by self or others)
*writing down reasons why one does **not** deserve to be punished (e.g. responsibility for abuse suffered)*
redirecting anger outwards

Managing the urge to self-injure:

putting self-injury off for an hour, a day, etc. (may find urge has gone later)
taking oneself away from access to objects used for self-injury
going to a safe place (e.g. to be with other people)
distraction: reading, exercise, activity involving concentration

Chapter 5

Some particular concerns in working with self-injury

Should I try to stop the person injuring themselves?

It is our experience that there is little to be gained in the long run by trying to prevent someone against their will from injuring themselves, or indeed by pressurising, persuading, or coercing them into stopping self-injury. Some of the reasons for this are:

- if the person still feels the need to self-injure they will find ways of doing so eventually anyway, but more secretly and perhaps more severely

- if they do not have other effective coping strategies then removing this means of coping may be dangerous

- trust in the professionals involved will be undermined

- the person may be made to feel that they are 'bad', out of control, not capable of being responsible for themselves

- they will probably also feel powerless, frightened and angry, which will lead them to need to self-injure even more

- their own ambivalence about their self-injury may be masked as they are forced into a polarised position. They are forced to identify either as the 'good patient' who agrees that self-injury is bad and promises never to do it again, or as the 'rebel' who is determined to injure themselves whatever. This will seriously undermine their ability to take responsibility for making decisions and choices about their own self-injury.

Human rights

We believe coercing someone not to hurt themselves to be an invasion and abuse of people's rights, especially given some of the methods involved. These might include: compulsory admission to hospital and treatment with drugs or ECT against their will; placing them under continuous observation; searching and confiscating their possessions; in secure environments, putting them into strip cells;[1] excluding them from services unless they comply; and forcing them to sign 'contracts' (which always seem to be completely one-sided, with all the obligations involved applying solely to the client).

The emotional harm which such actions may do to the person (especially given the likelihood that at least some of them will be highly reminiscent of childhood abuse suffered) also needs to be weighed against the damage which the person's continued self-injury may do. In many cases, the injuries involved are not severe and the means used to prevent them are unjustifiably intrusive and potentially more harmful.

---

[1] *Sadly, it is not uncommon for individuals in psychiatric and secure hospitals to request or apparently welcome such treatment. Their usual justification for this is that they wish to be 'kept safe'. As this implies that they do not in fact wish to injure themselves, it seems that this would be an ideal time to explore with them ways they can avoid self-injury, while retaining dignity, responsibility and control. It may also be that they have other motivations, such as wishing to communicate how desperate they are, to obtain much-needed attention and support, and so on. In this event, it would clearly be preferable to try to meet their needs without resorting to treatment which is unnecessarily oppressive (and demanding, in terms of staff time).*

Having said all this, there will be times for some workers in some agencies when they feel they are compelled to intervene, because of their responsibility for an individual's safety. It is important to be realistic about this. Fear of accountability may lead workers to panic about quite minor self-injury, when in fact their legal and professional responsibility applies only to death or serious injury.

(It is for managers to establish what their agency's responsibility is and to incorporate this in a clear policy and guidelines. More will be said about this in Chapter 6.)

Negotiation

Even where staff feel that they must intervene in a person's self-injury, they should try to negotiate with their patient or client, rather than simply being coercive. Many people, given the chance and a proper explanation, will understand the position of a worker or agency with responsibility and concern for their safety. Many will be willing to negotiate with workers in order to keep their self-injury within acceptable limits. They may be prepared to accept certain restrictions, if they have a say in these.

"I can understand them taking away my blades, if they'd just leave me in my own room. I'd be okay then. It's being put in strips: you feel so scared and degraded, you're just even more desperate. You have to find some way of hurting yourself when they put you in there."

"I told the staff that I wanted to be left alone if I just cut myself, but that I wanted them to stop me if I burned, because that could get really bad.. I might argue at the time, but it's what I want really. They accepted that."

Residential and inpatient settings

A number of particular issues arise in residential settings (such as hostels, refuges, children's homes, etc.), inpatient and secure settings.

(Some of the same issues may also arise in other group settings, such as day hospitals, drop-in centres, etc., and this section may also be of interest to those working in such settings.)

- Reactions of other residents.
  Self-injury on the part of some clients can be very difficult for other residents, who may feel upset, angry, jealous, responsible, and so on. They may react to these feelings by rejecting and ridiculing the person who self-injures, or sometimes by beginning to injure themselves.

- An atmosphere of unpredictability, anxiety and chaos.

- Difficulties with staffing.
  Where staff find themselves spending a lot of time responding to the distress and wounds of someone who injures themselves, other areas of their work and the needs of other residents may get pushed to one side.

- Competitiveness between residents who self-injure.

- Staff stress.

"Not knowing when it's going to happen, what someone is going to do, trying to be there for people when you have so much to do - it's such a strain."

"I know this sounds awful but I sometimes think I don't care what they do so long as it's not on my shift."

There are a number of ways in which staff can tackle these issues:

Preparation

Where someone who self-injures is to join a residential setting, planning is important. Staffing levels should be adequate to support all residents, even where self-injury imposes extra demands. Where possible, it is a good idea for the prospective resident to visit in advance and to talk through what their needs and wants are in relation to self-injury. Staff can also explain any policy on self-injury or talk with the person about their concerns (for safety, etc.) They can explore how best the client and staff can work together. (This can also be done on admission if a prior visit is not possible.)

Staff should work out how they are to respond to the person's possible self-injury. If there is not already a policy and guidelines in place, staff could think at this point about some of the things suggested in considering policy in Chapter 6.

Some residential projects involve existing residents in meetings concerning admission of new people. Even if they have no involvement in decisions, it is a good idea to talk with existing residents or patients about self-injury. This can help them to accept, cope with and support a new person who self-injures.

It is important that workers support other service users and that self-injury and its impact are talked about with the group as a whole. People are usually able to relax about self-injury if they understand that it is just one way of coping. (It may help for them to discuss their own ways.) They need to know that staff can handle self-injury and will not see them as less upset or important than a person who hurts themselves.

Supporting a resident who self-injures

It is important that a resident who self-injures knows what support is available to them, especially when they are distressed. It helps greatly if people know that there are regular and reliable opportunities for them to talk with a worker about their feelings and experiences - such as planned sessions with a keyworker. They also need to feel that there are goals to their treatment or placement, and that they themselves have a say in setting and reviewing these goals.

A person who self-injures also needs to be able to ask for support at moments of crisis. This will not only help them to sometimes avoid self-injury, but also (more importantly) to learn that they can communicate and deal with their distress by talking. Ideally, support should be available whenever the person needs it, not just when they have hurt themselves or when they feel the urge to self-injure. People need to learn that their feelings and needs will be taken seriously without their having to hurt themselves.

It can take a long time and a lot of courage for someone to learn to identify and verbalise their feelings and to ask for support. In the meantime, support should also be given when they do hurt themselves.

Clearly, with the best will in the world staff cannot be available at every moment for every person. Different residents may need varying amounts of support at different times, but there may be (many!) times when the sum of the group's needs is greater than that to which staff can respond. Where staff feel persistently overburdened, individuals who do not articulate their needs as dramatically as people who self-injure may be neglected and feel resentful. Some may start to injure themselves. Staff (and residents) may become angry and punitive towards a resident who frequently self-injures or threatens to do so, and seems 'too demanding'.

There are a number of ways of helping this situation:

- Staffing levels may need to be increased. It is particularly important to maintain adequate staffing levels during times of the day when self-injury seems to increase - usually in the evening.

- Limitations on staffing and support should be acknowledged and discussed, rather than individuals who self-injure being scapegoated.

- Residents may be able to share more support with each other, and ways of promoting this (perhaps through more groupwork, 'buddying' schemes, etc.) could be explored.

- Residents can be helped to develop ways of coping and expressing themselves which do not require the immediate involvement of staff. Many possibilities listed in the previous section (pages 48 and 49) may be relevant. Staff should, however, be sure to acknowledge the ways a person has supported and expressed themselves.

Dealing with injuries

In residential and inpatient settings there may be repeated instances of self-injury, perhaps on the part of several clients at any one time. This can lead to staff spending a lot of time reactively dealing with injuries, while other areas of their work are pushed aside.

In our view it is helpful for people who self-injure to take as much responsibility as they can cope with for dealing with their own injuries. Often injuries are minor, and people can care adequately for them if they are provided with a first aid kit and some simple instruction. (They may still need some emotional support and should not simply be abandoned or ignored.) It is a good idea for staff to try to foster relationships with GP's and A&E staff, so that they are more ready to respond supportively to residents needing treatment for more severe injuries.

'Contagion'

Where residents or patients first begin to self-injure following admission, seemingly 'copying' others, a number of possibilities exist:

- the self-injury may be an individual's response to anxiety, distress, loss, disorientation, powerlessness, or many other feelings induced by being in the new environment
- it may be or seem that self-injury is the unofficial norm, 'language' or 'currency' in the unit
- self-injury may be a way of trying to belong or prove oneself in the group
- residents may perceive that their distress and needs are not seen unless they injure themselves
- self-injury in the client group may be a signal of unsatisfactory aspects of their environment or treatment, or a response to conflict amongst staff
- self-injury may be a means of rebellion by residents against the power and authority of staff and the agency.

Clearly the first priority is to understand what is going on. The uncomfortable possibility needs to be considered that the agency or staff themselves are doing something to foster the proliferation of self-injury. Staff need to talk with residents, individually and as a group, to find out what they see as the reasons for the self-injury. Given the opportunity to be heard sympathetically and taken seriously, many residents will be prepared to voice problems and address issues for the group, and to be creative in finding solutions.

"It gets on my nerves when staff say that you're copying. It's not that, it's that you get so wound up in here and there's nothing else you can do with it."

Ways of guarding against or addressing the problem of 'rashes' or 'contagion' include:

- Ensuring that all residents have the attention and support they need.

- Treating all residents with respect, as people with rights, views, abilities and strengths.

- Encouraging direct verbal expression of feelings, conflicts and difficulties, by individuals and the group, and between residents and staff.

- Fostering a culture of mutual support and co-operation, both within the client group and between residents and staff.

- Giving residents as much say as possible in their own lives and in the circumstances and running of their present environment.

- Providing safe channels through which grievances can be reported and properly followed up.

- Ensuring that residents/patients have access to sufficient stimulating, purposeful activities and opportunities for social contact. (Boredom and isolation can foster self-injury. Evenings may be a particular problem.)

- Providing opportunities for individuals to safely discharge anger, tension and frustration, e.g. a punchbag, sports.

Young people

Much, if not all that has been said in this book can be applied to work with children and young people who self-injure, as much as to work with adults. However, a number of particular issues need to be considered in working with youngsters:

- The likelihood that self-injury will reflect current (or very recent) issues in their lives which need to be dealt with, such as abuse or bullying.

- The possible limits placed on confidentiality in services by child protection responsibilities. These need to be established clearly and communicated honestly to young people approaching a service.

- The possibility that lack of knowledge and experience, recklessness, bravado, etc. may cause a young person to injure themselves more severely than they might really wish or intend. It may be especially important for workers to help young people learn about safety issues in respect of self-injury.

- Greater concern about legal liability and responsibility of workers for the young person's safety. This needs to be addressed in policy-making and supervision.

- The difficulty of making contact with and engaging some vulnerable young people in services, and the likelihood that they may react strongly in opposition to workers perceived as adopting an authoritarian approach.

Young people need to be treated with respect and sensitivity and to be allowed choices and control. In the short term this may conflict with concerns for their safety when self-injury is an issue. In the longer term, however, such treatment can lead to a better chance that they will build and maintain a good alliance with helpers.

- The need for self-injury to be tackled before it becomes entrenched behaviour. This conflicts with a tendency for adults coming into contact with young people not to take their self-injury seriously, regarding it as a 'craze' or 'phase', 'copying', or 'attention-seeking'. This means that the young person may not be taken seriously and referred to or given information about much-needed sources of help. Workers having regular contact with youngsters, such as teachers, youth workers, residential care staff, etc. can help by being aware of self-injury and responding to signs that a young person may be in trouble.

- The importance of peer groups to young people. This may make it more likely that self-injury will be adopted as a 'language', a means of belonging or rebellion, etc. (but see pages 57-58 on this issue). A related point is the possibility that youngsters may imitate self-injury by musicians or others they admire. It is unlikely that they will do this persistently or severely unless they have serious underlying difficulties of their own.

- The strength of peer group ties and norms can be valuable, if appropriately channelled and supported. They can result in a great deal of positive mutual support and encouragement to individuals wishing to tackle their self-injury and underlying problems.

- The lack of services (especially residential services, but also day provision, counselling, etc.) for young people which are able and willing to cope supportively with self-injury. This means that youngsters may be referred inappropriately to adult services (especially psychiatric and secure settings) in which they are very vulnerable and which do not really meet their needs. The needs of young people in adult services must be met more appropriately, while agencies providing services for youngsters should be better prepared and trained to deal with self-injury.

People with learning difficulties

It can be very distressing for staff and carers to witness repeated self-injury by someone with learning difficulties, feeling powerless to understand why this is happening and what is needed to stop it. People with learning difficulties who self-injure may do so for a range of reasons:

The same reasons as people who are not learning disabled: to cope with and express painful experiences and feelings. Particular attention needs to be paid to the possibility that a learning disabled person may be distressed due to circumstances in their current life, but that this has not been apparent. (Examples include abuse, problems in relationships, loneliness, bereavement, illness or discomfort, etc.)

Communication: Where a learning disabled person has difficulties with communication, self-injury may be an attempt to signal that something is wrong or a need is not being met. It might also be a means of dealing with the frustration caused by their difficulties with communication. Staff and carers may need to be extremely sensitive, patient and creative in developing ways in which the person can communicate their feelings and needs, otherwise self-injury (which is often in fact quite an effective means of gaining a response) will continue.

Lack of stimulation: A person with a learning (or physical or sensory) disability may not get enough sensory, mental or social stimulation, particularly if they are not able to seek out these things successfully for themselves. Their needs for sex and intimacy may also be frustrated. Someone in this situation may self-injure repeatedly as a way of experiencing **something** - banging one's head being perhaps preferable to a sensory vacuum. People with long histories of severe self-injury have been enabled to stop harming themselves when sufficient sensory stimulation, purposeful activity and interaction with others were provided.

It may take considerable work, patience and commitment to help someone with severe learning difficulties and long-standing self-harming behaviour to respond to new stimuli and to efforts to interact with them.

Powerlessness: Depending on their living situation, it may be difficult for a learning disabled person to experience themselves as exerting much control or autonomy in their lives. Self-injury may then be a means of feeling a sense of control or agency. It might also be a way of trying to protest or exert some influence over one's situation. Advocacy may help, as will efforts to allow the person to have as much say as possible in their lives and circumstances.

Organic disease: A proportion of learning disabled people who self-injure are believed to do so because of organic disease (see Walsh & Rosen, 1988) and clearly this needs to be investigated. However, it is likely that this proportion is smaller than has often been assumed, and that most self-injury is a response to environmental factors.

Chapter 6
Support for effective working

Anyone who works with people who self-injure, or indeed with people in any emotional distress, needs guidance and support for their work. There are a number of important things which agencies can provide which will help staff to work effectively with people who self-injure without themselves becoming overburdened or distressed:

- Policies, procedures and guidelines
- Training
- Back-up
- Supervision and support
- Networking

Policies, procedures and guidelines

Few agencies have any clear, defined policy on dealing with self-injury. This means that staff are left to flounder and may feel very unsure or anxious. Their responses to self-injury may be founded on inadequate information, or on impressions they have picked up about how self-injury is dealt with. There may be variations in responses to self-injury between different staff, so that clients feel anxious and may try to play staff off against each other. Different clients may also be treated differently, which can be confusing, distressing and divisive.

In the absence of policy and guidance, staff are likely to become more concerned with 'watching their own backs', at the expense of consideration of their clients' needs for such things as privacy, choice and responsibility.

On the other hand, a well thought-out policy and guidance on dealing with self-injury can support and free staff to work confidently and creatively.

The sorts of things which a policy and associated procedures and guidelines need to cover are:

Philosophy: what is the organisation's understanding of and philosophy concerning self-injury? How does it see its own role in relation to people who self-injure?

Use of/admission to service: are any restrictions to be placed on use of the service by people who self-injure? (For example, a residential project may realistically decide it can only properly provide for the needs of a limited number of individuals who self-injure at any one time.)

Confidentiality: under what, if any circumstances would concern about self-injury be considered to take priority over confidentiality (e.g. would a worker be expected / permitted to call an ambulance against a client's will?) It should also be clear what support / advice is available to a worker having to make such decisions.

Responding: how will staff respond to:
- someone who discloses or has a history of self-injury
- someone who says they feel like hurting themselves now
- someone who has just injured themselves (the person as well as the injuries).

Safety:
- how are people who self-injure helped to keep themselves safe (e.g. access to first aid equipment)
- are any restrictions placed on clients' access to objects which may be used for self-injury?

Other service-users and staff:
- how will other service users be supported in sharing the service with people who self-injure?
- what training, information, supervision and support will be given to staff dealing with self-injury?
- how can the potential distress caused by self-injury be minimised (e.g. people who self-injure can be asked to do this in the privacy of their own room, etc.)

Reporting: are staff required to report self-injury to anyone else within or outside the agency? Is self-injury recorded?

Policies and procedures need to be devised through discussion involving management and staff at all levels, and preferably also service users. (Service users should, we believe, have a real and respected say in how they are to be treated. They are also likely to be able to provide extremely valuable input in devising workable and helpful policy.)

The possible implications of all policy proposals need to be fully explored. Policies and procedures must be realistic and workable, so that staff and clients feel committed to working within them. An example of an unrealistic policy (and one which is often reflected in Care plans which all concerned realise have little hope of success) may be to eliminate all self-injury amongst patients/clients within a short time following admission. A more realistic policy might involve aiming to work with clients to help them gradually contain their self-injury within reasonably safe limits.

Once policies and procedures have been agreed and drawn up they need to be communicated to staff, with briefing/training provided to guide implementation. Relevant aspects of the policies should also be communicated in an appropriate way to service users. There need to be regular opportunities for staff and users to give feedback and to review the working and usefulness of such policies.

Training

The precise content of training will depend on the agency and the roles of staff concerned. Training most usefully includes some or all of the following topics:

Staff's attitudes and feelings about self-injury

Information about the nature, incidence, etc. of self-injury

Self-injury as one of many more or less 'self-harming' coping methods

Myths and misconceptions about self-injury

Why people self-injure

What is helpful/unhelpful in service responses; implications for workers in the appropriate setting(s)

Implementing agency policies and guidelines

Managing the impact of self-injury on other service-users, families, staff

Staff support/supervision needs and opportunities

Resources - relevant local and national services, literature

In certain settings (as appropriate): Risk assessment; Care planning; Harm reduction

It is important that this is provided by trainers who have a wide knowledge and understanding of what self-injury is all about. It is also important that they should understand how your particular agency operates and have wide experience of direct work with different client groups.

Back-up

It is essential that staff working with people who self-injure know that they are backed up not just by policies and procedures but by their colleagues and most importantly by their managers. Staff need to be able to call on others for advice and support. They are operating in an area of risk and they need to know that they will not be scapegoated or left to 'carry the can' alone if clients in their care continue to self-injure, or indeed come to significant harm.

Supervision and support

All workers having significant contact with people who self-injure need support and perhaps formal supervision. These things are not a luxury or a sign that staff are not competent or able to cope. They are a pre-requisite for effective and professional working. It is our experience from training many groups of workers that very few feel they have adequate support, and they recognise that they themselves as well as their work with clients suffer as a result. Lack of funds and time are usually cited as the reasons for this inadequacy. There is a clear need for agencies to pay greater attention to the support and supervision needs of staff and to be creative in finding ways of responding to these, even where resources are limited.

Precisely what forms of support are needed will vary according to the person's particular role, but elements of what is needed may include some or all of the following:

Contact with other workers: Some professionals work alone or have little chance to spend time with colleagues. At the very least workers need opportunities to meet and be with others who share similar work.

Offloading: Opportunities to let off steam, to talk about the difficult issues and feelings which are being brought up by working with self-injury.

Recognition: Acknowledgement and appreciation for the difficulties being tackled and the efforts and progress being made.

Sharing ideas: The chance to discuss the work with others, bouncing around ideas and gaining new insights.

Support in the work itself: For example in a situation where a client needs a high level of contact and care it is probably best if other people can share the load.

Case discussion: Those doing in-depth work with clients who self-injure will need regular opportunities to reflect in more detail on the process and content of their work and any difficulties arising. This may be needed by teams working together as well as by individual practitioners.

Self-awareness: Opportunities to reflect honestly on feelings and reactions to working with people who self-injure and to become aware of how these affect the work. This may also lead to a recognition that we need support to tackle distress of our own which is being triggered by work with clients.

Some possible ways of providing these elements include:

Teamworking

Responsibility for working with clients who self-injure may most usefully be shared within small multi-disciplinary teams. These will benefit by regularly planning and reviewing their work together, and can provide each other with on-going support.

"I couldn't cope with this work on my own. We all share the load."

Regular staff / team meetings

Staff groups and teams can meet together regularly, within work time, to share support and discuss issues of concern.

It can be helpful to appoint an informal 'facilitator' for each meeting who will ensure that the group maintains its focus on staff support rather than drifting into 'chat' about clients, administrative issues, holidays, etc.!

Where time is a problem it is important to be creative. It is often more possible than first appears for staff groups to take time out for such meetings. For example, on one specialist unit for severe self-harmers the whole staff team takes an hour away from patients each day, trusting patients to be able to take responsibility and support one another in their absence.

Peer support groups

A variation on the above idea is to set up smaller groups of people, not necessarily those from the same team, who wish to meet together for mutual support.

Supervision

Supervision should provide a regular opportunity for a practitioner to:

- review and reflect on the content, process and progress of their work with clients

- discuss plans for aspects of future work

- explore their own feelings and responses to their clients (and to issues such as self-injury), identifying the possible impact of these on the work and ways of dealing with this

- explore concerns and dilemmas concerning ethical issues, relationships with other workers, etc.

- identify any personal issues triggered by or affecting the work which may need to be addressed further elsewhere.

Supervision by line managers

In many agencies supervision is given by line managers. This can be satisfactory, and has the advantage that the manager can become aware of issues which need to be addressed, such as the organisation and allocation of work, staff support, and so on.

A number of problems can also arise where line managers provide supervision. Personalities may not match. The manager may have insufficient recent experience of the type of work being carried out by the supervisee. Staff may not feel safe to be frank about their difficulties in their work with someone who is probably also responsible for appraisal, discipline, promotion decisions, etc. Neither may they feel easy about mentioning personal issues which may be triggered by or affecting the work. It may be difficult for a manager who is used to the same circumstances and methods of working to help the worker towards fresh insights or ways forward. And often other areas of managers' work are given priority over supervision, so that it is provided only infrequently and erratically.

It may be preferable for supervision to be provided by another senior or experienced staff member, rather than by an individual's direct line manager. Many people also feel they would prefer to have supervision from someone outside the organisation within which they work.

Where line managers do provide supervision, the following may help make the supervision relationship more comfortable and useful:

- Supervision needs to be given importance and to be allocated regular, uninterrupted time in a room where privacy is assured.

- Supervisees need to be given clear information on the role of supervision, what issues it is seen as appropriate to bring, confidentiality, and the boundaries between this and other aspects of the working relationship.

- Managers and others providing supervision should be trained in supervision skills.

- Within the supervision there should be an emphasis on validation of the supervisee's work and skills, together with co-exploration of problems and possible solutions. Managers should guard against adopting a critical, authoritarian or 'expert' position.

Peer supervision

Supervision of one another by work colleagues may be an economical and convenient means of ensuring staff get some support and feedback on their work. It has some of the same advantages and drawbacks as supervision by line managers. An additional benefit may be that a colleague may have greater familiarity with the work being supervised. On the other hand, colleagues may be too immersed in similar difficulties to be able to offer fresh perspectives, or even to give much support.

One difficulty is that peers may not feel they have 'permission' to question and perhaps challenge each other in ways which would enable them to get the best out of the supervision.

Peer supervision works best if an appropriate model for the sessions (process and content) is established and training is given in how to carry out and use this form of supervision. One useful but still fairly economical approach to supervision might be to intersperse regular individual peer supervision sessions with less frequent group sessions led by a manager, senior colleague or external supervisor.

External supervision

Supervision from an independent, external supervisor can be very helpful for a number of reasons:

- The supervisee will probably feel less anxious about betraying her 'inadequacies', doubts, feelings, personal difficulties, etc.

- The supervisor may be able to bring a fresh perspective to bear.

- It can be very validating for the supervisee to feel that their work is seen and recognised in the world outside their workplace.

- The supervisor will be (or should be!) experienced and skilled in the supervisory role.

- It is possible to 'shop around' for a supervisor who has knowledge and experience around all the issues and circumstances the worker has to deal with.

"Going to my supervisor often makes me feel better about my work - the chance to stand back and really think about what I'm doing, instead of just being immersed in it. Recognising what I'm doing well, and working out what's going wrong. I'm sure it helps me to be more confident and professional."

Possible drawbacks of using an external supervisor include lack of familiarity with the worker's organisation and possibly with their work role and the demands this makes upon them. Supervisors often come from a counselling or therapy background and some may have little or no experience of the statutory or voluntary sectors, or of particular roles within these. Having said this, the supervisor may still be able to grasp the difficulties and issues which the worker brings and to offer considerable help. The supervisor should have knowledge and understanding of self-injury, and should hold attitudes towards it which are compatible with or respectful towards those of the worker.

Group supervision

Group supervision may be particularly valuable for dealing with issues raised by self-injury for the following reasons:

- The opportunity for sharing of feelings and difficulties experienced in working with self-injury will encourage the development of mutual support within the work situation.

- Group supervision can provide the opportunity for staff to voice and address disagreement about how self-injury should be viewed and treated.

- Issues which need to be further debated and/or dealt with through policy may be identified.

- Issues within the agency or between staff which may be fostering self-injury (e.g. in residential settings) may be brought out.

Clearly, group supervision cannot provide full attention to all the individual cases or responses of each worker, and the best model may be to provide a combination of individual and group supervision, at appropriate intervals.

Networking

Contact with workers in other agencies may be especially helpful for those working with an issue as distressing and poorly understood as self-injury. It is particularly valuable for those working alone or in very small projects.

Workers from different agencies can share support as well as information and ideas about the work, resources, etc. It is important for those working in different sectors, disciplines and settings to compare their understanding and experiences of working with self-injury. This will aid the development of better models for working, as well as fostering better co-operation between agencies and professionals. Networking groups can also organise and share the cost of specialised training on self-injury.

A number of groups of professionals in different parts of the country have begun to set up interest groups for those working with self-injury, and have received an enthusiastic response. Practitioners in other areas could consider doing something similar, perhaps advertising in local newsletters concerning mental health or related issues. The Self-injury Forum is a national network which has been set up to co-ordinate some of these initiatives and to provide a means of sharing information, ideas and support. (Address at back of book.)

"I know this work can be hard and frustrating at times, but when you get together with like-minded people you realise you really are making a difference. This makes it feel worthwhile."

References

Arnold, L. (1995) *Women & Self-injury: A survey of 76 women.* Bristol Crisis Service for Women.

Arnold, L. & Babiker, G. (1997) *The Language of Injury.* British Psychological Society.

Arnold, L & Magill, A. (1997) *What's The Harm? A book for young people who self-harm*; (1998) *The Self-harm Help Book*

Burstow, B. (1992) *Radical Feminist Therapy.* Sage.

Harrison, D. (1996) *Vicious Circles.* Good Practices in Mental Health.

Pembroke, L. (Ed.). (1994) *Self Harm: Perspectives from Personal Experience.* London: Survivors Speak Out.

Potier, M. (1993) Giving Evidence: Women's Lives in Ashworth Maximum Security Hospital. *Feminism and Psychology*, 3(3).

Spandler, H. (1996) *Who's Hurting Who?* 42nd St, Manchester.

Tantam, D & Whittaker, J. (1992) Personality Disorder and Self-wounding. *British Journal of Psychiatry*, 161, 451-464.

Van der Kolk, et al. (1991) Childhood Origins of self-destructive Behaviour. *American Journal of Psychiatry*, 148(12), 1665-1671.

Walsh, B. W. & Rosen, P. M. (1988) *Self-Mutilation: Theory, Research and Treatment.* New York: Guilford Press.

Resources

Basement Project PO Box 5 Abergavenny NP7 5XW 01873 856524 Website: freespace.virgin.net/basement.project

Bristol Crisis Service for Women PO Box 654 Bristol Helpline 0117 925 1119

National Self-harm Network PO Box 16190 London NW1 3WW

Appendix: Notes on NICE Guidelines

The following are some of the key priorities from the NICE guideline* for GP's and Hospital Emergency staff in treating people who self-harm (pp 5-6):

People who have self-harmed should be treated with the same care, respect and privacy as any patient. In addition, healthcare professionals should take full account of the likely distress associated with self-harm.

Clinical and non-clinical staff who have contact with people who self-harm in any setting should be provided with appropriate training to equip them to understand and care for people who have self-harmed.

If a person who has self-harmed has to wait for treatment, he or she should be offered an environment that is safe, supportive and minimises any distress. For many patients, this may be a separate, quiet room with supervision and regular contact with a named member of staff to ensure safety.

People who have self-harmed should be offered treatment for the physical consequences of self-harm, regardless of their willingness to accept psychosocial assessment or psychiatric treatment.

Adequate anaesthesia and/or analgesia should be offered to people who have self-injured throughout the process of suturing or other painful treatments.

Staff should provide full information about the treatment options, and make all efforts necessary to ensure that someone who has self-harmed can give, and has the opportunity to give, meaningful and informed consent before any and each procedure (for example, taking the person to hospital by ambulance) or treatment is initiated.

Ref: Self-harm: The short-term physical and psychological management and secondary prevention of self-harm in primary and secondary care. Guideline 16, July 2004 National Institute for Clinical Excellence, Mid City Place, 71 High Holborn London WC1V 6NA. www.nice.org.uk

Discussion

These key priorities reflect some of the principles the Basement Project has been campaigning for during the last decade. We therefore endorse them. It is clear that the Guideline Development Group have worked hard to produce guidelines which will significantly improve the response to and treatment of people who self-harm. We hope that such principles will increasingly be reflected in services. There are some parts of the Guideline about which we have reservations, particularly those concerning psychiatric assessment and issues of consent to treatment.

While it is stated that *'self-harm is an expression of personal distress, not an illness, and there are many varied reasons for a person to harm him or herself'* (p. 7) there seems to be a contradictory emphasis on psychiatric assessment. The issue of consent is seen as important and the following statement assumes the capacity to give consent: *'In the assessment and treatment of people who have self-harmed, mental capacity should be assumed unless there is evidence to the contrary'* (p.11). However, this is preceded by a recommendation that *'all healthcare professionals who have contact, in the emergency situation, with people who have self-harmed should be adequately trained to assess mental capacity and to make decisions about when treatment and care can be given without consent'* (p.11).

We are concerned that the emphasis on psychiatric assessment and the possibility of compulsory treatment may lead to a heavy-handed approach which would not be in accordance with the previously quoted Key Priorities. It is such an approach which has often led people who self-harm to avoid contact with services. Where there is any possibility of treatment being given without consent, we would like at least to see a requirement to provide an advocate or legal advisor to the patient.